HISTORY ON THE HIGH SEAS

ABOARD THE TITANIC

BY ELIZABETH KRAJNIK

Gareth Stevens PUBLISHING

Please visit our website, www.garethstevens.com. For a free color catalog of all our high-quality books, call toll free 1-800-542-2595 or fax 1-877-542-2596.

Library of Congress Cataloging-in-Publication Data

Names: Krajnik, Elizabeth.
Title: Aboard the Titanic / Elizabeth Krajnik.
Description: New York : Gareth Stevens Publishing, 2020. | Series: History on the high seas | Includes glossary and index.
Identifiers: ISBN 9781538238028 (pbk.) | ISBN 9781538238042 (library bound) | ISBN 9781538238035 (6 pack)
Subjects: LCSH: Titanic (Steamship)–Juvenile literature. | Shipwrecks–North Atlantic Ocean–History–20th century–Juvenile literature. | Disasters–North Atlantic Ocean–History–20th century–Juvenile literature.
Classification: LCC G530.T6 K73 2020 | DDC 910.9163'4–dc23

First Edition

Published in 2020 by
Gareth Stevens Publishing
111 East 14th Street, Suite 349
New York, NY 10003

Designer: Katelyn E. Reynolds
Editor: Therese Shea

Photo credits: Cover, p. 1 Culture Club/Getty Images; cover, pp. 1–24 (porthole and wood background) Andrey_Kuzmin/Shutterstock.com; cover, pp. 1–24 (wood sign) ESB Professional/Shutterstock.com; cover, pp. 1–24 (brass plate) photocell/Shutterstock.com; pp. 2–24 (old paper) Kostenko Maxim/Shutterstock.com; pp. 4–24 (old notebook) BrAt82/Shutterstock.com; p. 5 (map) 10topvector/Shutterstock.com; p. 5 (inset) http://students.umf.maine.edu/~hartwenr/webquest/teacherpage/titanic%20in%20dock.jpg/Soerfm/Wikipedia.org; p. 7 (main) Library of Congress/Kekator/Wikipedia.org; p. 7 (inset) Szajci/Wikipedia.org; p. 9 Martin Rickett - PA Images/PA Images via Getty Images; p. 11 (main) The Print Collector/Getty Images; p. 11 (inset) Library of Congress/Soerfm/Getty Images; p. 13 Universal Images Group/Getty Images; p. 15 Titanic Museum Attraction/Barcroft USA/Getty Images; p. 17 Leemage/UIG via Getty Images; p. 19 (main) George Rinhart/Corbis via Getty Images; p. 19 (inset) Universal History Archive/UIG via Getty Images; p. 21 (main) Ralph White/Corbis Documentary/Getty Images; p. 21 (inset) Dorling Kindersley/Getty Images.

Printed in the United States of America

CPSIA compliance information: Batch #CS19GS: For further information contact Gareth Stevens, New York, New York at 1-800-542-2595.

CONTENTS

WORDS IN THE GLOSSARY APPEAR IN **BOLD** TYPE THE FIRST TIME THEY ARE USED IN THE TEXT.

COME ABOARD THE *TITANIC*

The *Titanic* was a famous British liner, a ship similar to a modern **cruise** ship. It set sail from Southampton, England, on April 10, 1912, on its first voyage, or journey.

On the evening of April 10, the *Titanic* stopped in Cherbourg, France, to pick up more **passengers**. The next morning, it made a final stop in Queenstown (now called Cobh) in Ireland. From there, the *Titanic* continued on its **doomed** voyage across the Atlantic Ocean toward New York City. It was carrying about 2,200 people in all.

CREWMAN'S LOG

In this log, or record, you'll read about the Titanic's voyage and passengers from the point of view of a crew member. These writings are made up, but based on facts.

THE *TITANIC'S* DOOMED VOYAGE

the *Titanic* in Southampton

THE *TITANIC'S* FULL NAME WAS RMS *TITANIC*. RMS STANDS FOR "ROYAL MAIL SHIP," WHICH MEANS IT CARRIED BRITISH MAIL.

BUILDING AN "UNSINKABLE" SHIP

In the early 1900s, the White Star Line company wanted to build large ships that were comfortable and fast. The *Titanic* was one of these ships. A man named Thomas Andrews was its main **designer**.

Completed in 1912, the *Titanic* had 16 watertight compartments, which were sections that could be closed off if the body of the ship was harmed. Each section was supposed to contain water. This design was meant to stop the entire ship from taking in too much water and sinking.

CREWMAN'S LOG

Welcome aboard! Many people have said the Titanic is unsinkable, and I believe this to be true. I'm awaiting the ship's first voyage. Many people come to the docks just to see the ship!

THE *TITANIC* HAD **ACCOMMODATIONS** FOR FIRST-CLASS, SECOND-CLASS, AND THIRD-CLASS PASSENGERS. IT WAS THE LARGEST PASSENGER SHIP AT THAT TIME.

WHO'S ON BOARD?

Of the over 2,200 people on the *Titanic*, about 1,300 were passengers. These people were excited to take part in the ship's first voyage, including wealthy people. In fact, the ship was sometimes called the "Millionaire's Special."

But there were many kinds of passengers, and they paid different prices for their tickets. Many third-class passengers paid around $34, or about $880 today. First-class tickets started at about $146, or about $3,755 today. However, the most expensive rooms on the *Titanic* cost $2,560. That's more than $60,000 today!

CREWMAN'S LOG

A number of third-class passengers have told me how nice their accommodations are compared to other ships. Plus, they get food each day. Other ships make third-class passengers bring their own!

IT'S HARD TO KNOW EXACTLY HOW MANY PEOPLE WERE IN EACH CLASS. IT'S BELIEVED BY SOME THAT THERE WERE 324 FIRST-CLASS PASSENGERS, 284 SECOND-CLASS PASSENGERS, AND 709 THIRD-CLASS PASSENGERS. BELOW IS A FIRST-CLASS TICKET.

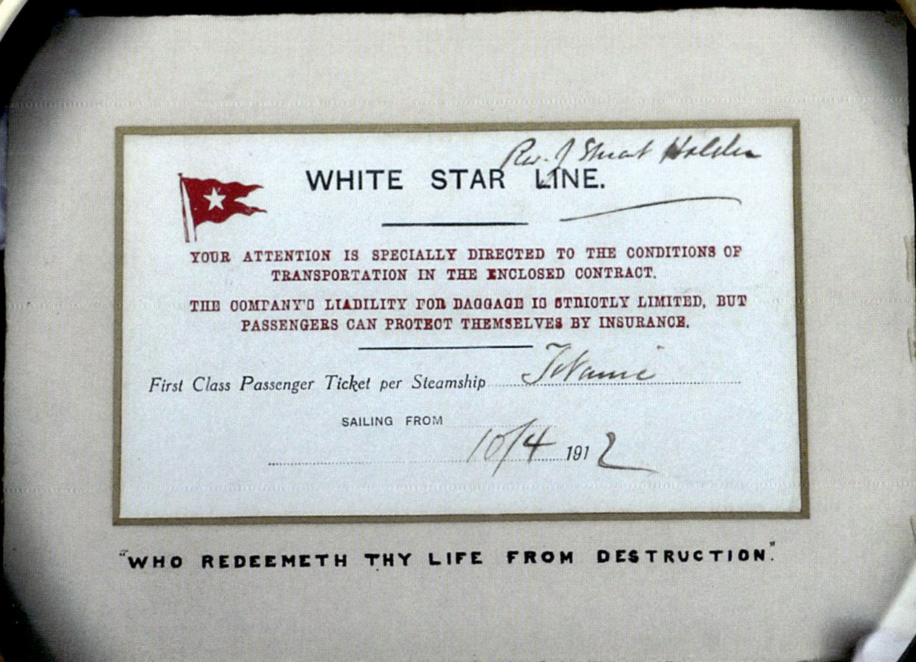

Rev. J Stuart Holden

WHITE STAR LINE.

YOUR ATTENTION IS SPECIALLY DIRECTED TO THE CONDITIONS OF TRANSPORTATION IN THE ENCLOSED CONTRACT.

THE COMPANY'S LIABILITY FOR BAGGAGE IS STRICTLY LIMITED, BUT PASSENGERS CAN PROTECT THEMSELVES BY INSURANCE.

First Class Passenger Ticket per Steamship Titanic

SAILING FROM

10/4 1912

"WHO REDEEMETH THY LIFE FROM DESTRUCTION".

TRAVELING FIRST CLASS

First-class accommodations were located in the upper decks. Each had several rooms, including a bathroom, and featured telephones, heaters, and fans for fresh air.

First-class passengers experienced comforts that had never been seen on other ocean liners. Their dining room was the largest of any ship. An **orchestra** played music while they ate. These passengers could play chess on deck or relax in a reading and writing room. There was a gym for exercise, as well as **squash** courts and even a swimming pool.

CREWMAN'S LOG

There are many wealthy people on board, including John Jacob Astor IV. I've seen him in the newspaper—I never thought I'd see him in real life. He's one of the richest people in the world!

FEATURES WHICH CONTRIBUTED TO THE SPLENDOURS OF THE TITANIC.

A SINGLE BERTH STATE-ROOM.

A DECK STATE ROOM.

THE SWIMMING BATH, A POPULAR FEATURE WHICH IS POSSESSED BY VERY FEW VESSELS AFLOAT.

THE TURKISH BATH COOLING ROOM, WHICH, WITH ITS SUGGESTION OF THE "MYSTERIOUS EAST," IS ONE OF THE SHIP'S MOST INTERESTING ROOMS.

THE VERANDAH CAFE ADJOINING THE SMOKE ROOM. IT IS SURROUNDED BY GREEN TRELLIS-WORK, OVER WHICH GROW CLIMBING PLANTS

THE MAIN STAIRCASE FROM THE ... UP AND DOWN TO E...

THE GEORGIAN SMOKE ROOM, PANELLED IN THE FINEST MAHOGANY AND RELIEVED EVERYWHERE WITH MOTHER-O'-PEARL INLAID WORK.

THE RESTAURANT, DECORATED ... FLOOR TO C...

THIS NEWSPAPER SHOWED SOME OF THE FIRST-CLASS FEATURES, INCLUDING THE SWIMMING POOL AND A GRAND STAIRCASE.

TRAVELING SECOND CLASS

Second-class passengers enjoyed comforts similar to first class on other ocean liners. They could walk on an outdoor walkway called a promenade. Tea and coffee were served to them in the library in the afternoon. Their dining room could seat around 2,400 people. Diners listened to piano music as they ate.

Along with two or four beds, second-class rooms featured desks and sinks. Their beds were made with clean sheets every day. However, second-class passengers had to share bathrooms with other passengers.

CREWMAN'S LOG

Most of our second-class passengers are Europeans who want to visit the United States. Some are people who work for first-class passengers. They ask me about the US, but I've never been there either!

PEOPLE WALK ON THE PROMENADE FOR SECOND-CLASS PASSENGERS ON THE *TITANIC*.

TRAVELING THIRD CLASS

The *Titanic*'s third-class passengers had the smallest living space. They were also closest to the ship's engines, which were very noisy. However, the *Titanic*'s third class was still considered comfortable compared to other ships' third class.

The third-class cabins were separated into an area for single women, an area for families, and an area for single men. There was a gathering space for all to enjoy. There was also a piano to play and listen to.

CREWMAN'S LOG

Some third-class passengers have to share their sleeping quarters with strangers. And there are only two bathtubs for all third-class passengers to use!

THIS IS A REPLICA, OR MODEL, OF A THIRD-CLASS CABIN. MOST THIRD-CLASS PASSENGERS WERE **IMMIGRANTS** HEADED TO AMERICA.

THE SINKING OF THE *TITANIC*

Passengers were only able to enjoy themselves for a short time. On the night of April 14, 1912, the *Titanic*'s side **scraped** against an iceberg, tearing it open. Many compartments that were supposed to be watertight filled with water.

Some blame the crewman operating the radio for **ignoring** an iceberg warning. The ship's lookouts were missing **binoculars** and didn't see the iceberg until too late. No matter the cause, the *Titanic* began sinking. Women and children were put into lifeboats first, but there wasn't enough room for everyone.

CREWMAN'S LOG

The orchestra played music while people got into the 20 lifeboats. No musicians got into the lifeboats. The captain and John Jacob Astor IV didn't make it into the lifeboats either.

THIS PICTURE FROM FRENCH NEWSPAPER *LE PETIT JOURNAL* SHOWS THE *TITANIC* STRIKING THE ICEBERG. HOWEVER, IT DIDN'T HIT IT STRAIGHT ON IN REAL LIFE.

RMS CARPATHIA

The RMS *Carpathia*, another British passenger liner, received one of *Titanic*'s **distress signals** at about 12:20 a.m. The *Carpathia*'s captain ordered the ship to head toward the *Titanic*. They got to the location at about 3:30 a.m., more than an hour after the *Titanic* had sunk. By then, about 1,500 people had died in the freezing waters of the Atlantic Ocean.

The *Carpathia* picked up the survivors in the lifeboats—about 705 people. Shortly after 9:00 a.m., the *Carpathia* set out for New York City. The ship arrived on April 18.

CREWMAN'S LOG

I was lucky to find a spot on a lifeboat. Many weren't so lucky. Most of those who died were crew and third-class passengers. We watched the Titanic break in two and sink.

PEOPLE WAITED IN THE STREETS OF NEW YORK CITY FOR THE ARRIVAL OF THE *TITANIC*'S SURVIVORS ABOARD THE *CARPATHIA*.

WHAT WENT WRONG?

A number of **investigations** were held to find out what had happened on the *Titanic*. Both the American and the British investigations concluded that the *Titanic* was traveling too fast. They also claimed that a nearby ship, the *Californian*, could have saved many lives if it had responded to the distress signals. Lack of lifeboats and safety training was also thought to have led to more lives lost.

The sunken ship wasn't found in the Atlantic until 1985. Even today, people are interested in the voyage of the *Titanic* and its sad end.

CREWMAN'S LOG

In the months after the sinking, people asked me questions about what happened that night. Many passengers didn't even know they were in danger until it was too late.

A LARGE SECTION OF THE *TITANIC* WAS RAISED IN 1998. SOME PEOPLE THOUGHT THE SHIP WAS A SEA GRAVE AND SHOULD HAVE BEEN LEFT ALONE.

GLOSSARY

accommodations: a place where travelers can sleep and find other services

binoculars: a tool that you hold up to your eyes and look through to see things that are far away

cruise: having to do with a journey on a ship to a number of places as a vacation

designer: one who plans how something new will look and work

distress signal: a call for help because of a dangerous situation, such as from a boat

doomed: having to do with very bad events that cannot be avoided

ignore: to do nothing about or in response to something or someone

immigrant: one who comes to a country to settle there

investigation: an ordered search for facts about something

orchestra: a group of musicians who play music together and who are led by a conductor

passenger: someone who rides on a plane, car, bus, or boat

scrape: to get damaged by rubbing against a hard or sharp surface

squash: a game played by two people with rackets and a rubber ball in a court with four walls

FOR MORE INFORMATION

Books

Caper, William. *Nightmare on the Titanic.* New York, NY: Bearport Publishing, 2019.

Dubowski, Mark. *Titanic: The Disaster That Shocked the World!* New York, NY: DK Publishing, 2015.

Sabol, Stephanie. *What Was the Titanic?* New York, NY: Penguin Workshop, 2018.

Websites

Remembering the Titanic
kids.nationalgeographic.com/explore/history/a-titanic-anniversary
Check out photographs and facts about the *Titanic.*

US History: The Titanic
ducksters.com/history/us_1900s/titanic.php
Read more about the *Titanic,* and take a quiz.

Publisher's note to educators and parents: Our editors have carefully reviewed these websites to ensure that they are suitable for students. Many websites change frequently, however, and we cannot guarantee that a site's future contents will continue to meet our high standards of quality and educational value. Be advised that students should be closely supervised whenever they access the internet.

INDEX